THE NATURE KIDS GUIDE TO
HIPPOS

DAVID ANDERSON

LP Media Inc. Publishing
Text copyright © 2026 by LP Media Inc.
All rights reserved.

For information address LP Media Inc. Publishing,
30012 Variolite St NW, Princeton MN 55371
www.lpmedia.org

Publication Data

Hippos
The Nature Kid's Guide to Hippos — First edition.

Summary: "Learn all about Hippos, the Nature Kid Way"
— Provided by publisher.

ISBN: 979-8-89818-093-5

[1. Hippos – Non-Fiction] I. Title.

Title: The Nature Kid's Guide to Hippos

CONTENTS

RIVER LIFE

Snort! A hippo floats in a cool river. Its big ears wiggle above the water.

Hippos live in Africa. They spend most of their day in rivers and lakes.

The water keeps hippos cool. Africa can be very hot, so hippos would get too warm on land all day.

Hippos like slow, calm water. They stand or walk in shallow spots. The water covers their big bodies, but their eyes, ears, and nostrils poke out above the surface.

Hippos can hold their breath for up to five minutes. They close their ears and nostrils tight underwater. Baby hippos can even nurse while submerged!

AFRICAN WATERS

Splash! A hippo walks into a wide lake in Africa. The water feels cool.

Hippos live in parts of eastern and southern Africa. They need water nearby to survive.

Hippos stay close to rivers, lakes, and swamps. They do not live in deserts or forests far from water.

Long ago, hippos lived in more places across Africa. Today, most are found in countries like Tanzania, Kenya, and Zambia.

Hippos can live in both freshwater and slightly salty water near the coast.

HUGE
HIPPOS

Thump! A hippo steps onto the riverbank. The ground shakes.

Hippos are very large animals. They are the third heaviest land animals on Earth. Only elephants and rhinos weigh more.

A male hippo can weigh up to 9,900 pounds. That is as heavy as a small car! Females are smaller, but still very big.

Hippos stand about five feet tall. Their big, round bodies are built for life in the water.

A hippo's head alone can weigh over 400 pounds. That is heavier than most adult humans.

BUILT BIG

Hippos cannot swim or float. They are too dense! They walk along river bottoms.

Grunt! A hippo opens its huge mouth wide. This animal is built big!

Hippos have bodies built for water life. Their legs are short and thick. This helps them walk on river bottoms.

A hippo's head is very large. Its mouth can open almost four feet wide! Big teeth and tusks fill the jaw.

Hippo skin is thick and smooth with no fur. Special glands make a pink, oily liquid. This acts like sunscreen.

Their eyes, ears, and nose sit on top of their head. This lets hippos see, hear, and breathe while mostly underwater.

SUPER SENSES

Swoosh! A hippo lifts its head from the water. Its ears twist and turn.

Hippos have strong senses. Their ears can move in different directions. This helps them hear sounds all around.

Their eyes also work well above and below water. They can spot danger quickly. Their nostrils close tight when they dive, too.

Underwater, hippos sense vibrations through their jaw. They feel movements in the water around them. This helps them know when other animals are near.

A clear membrane covers hippo eyes like goggles underwater.

TOUGH
TANKS

Rumble! A hippo stands its ground. Its thick body looks like armor.

Hippos have many ways to stay safe. Their huge size scares most predators away. Few animals want to fight something so big.

Hippo skin is about two inches thick in some spots. This tough hide protects them from bites and scratches.

Their large tusks are powerful weapons. These teeth can grow over a foot long. Hippos use them to fight off threats.

A hippo's bite force reaches 1,800 pounds—one of the strongest of any land animal.

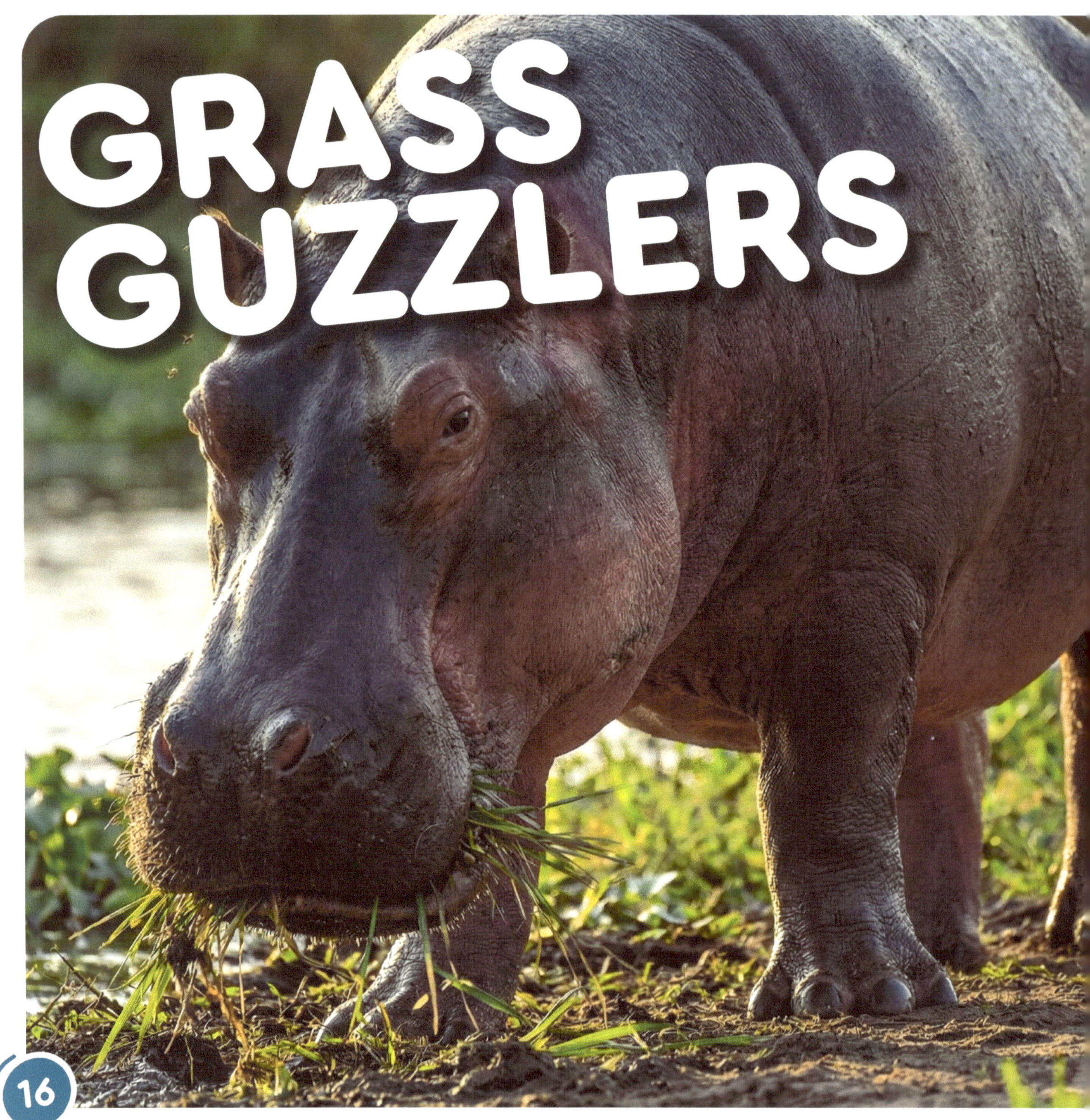
GRASS
GUZZLERS

Chomp! A hippo bites a big bunch of grass. Yum! Time for dinner!

Hippos eat mostly grass. They are herbivores, which means they mostly eat plants.

A hippo eats about 80 pounds of grass each night. That sounds like a lot! But it is not much for such a big animal.

Hippos use their wide lips to grab grass. They pull it right out of the ground. Then their flat back teeth grind the grass into mush.

Hippos swallow grass whole. They do not chew cud!

NIGHT NIBBLERS

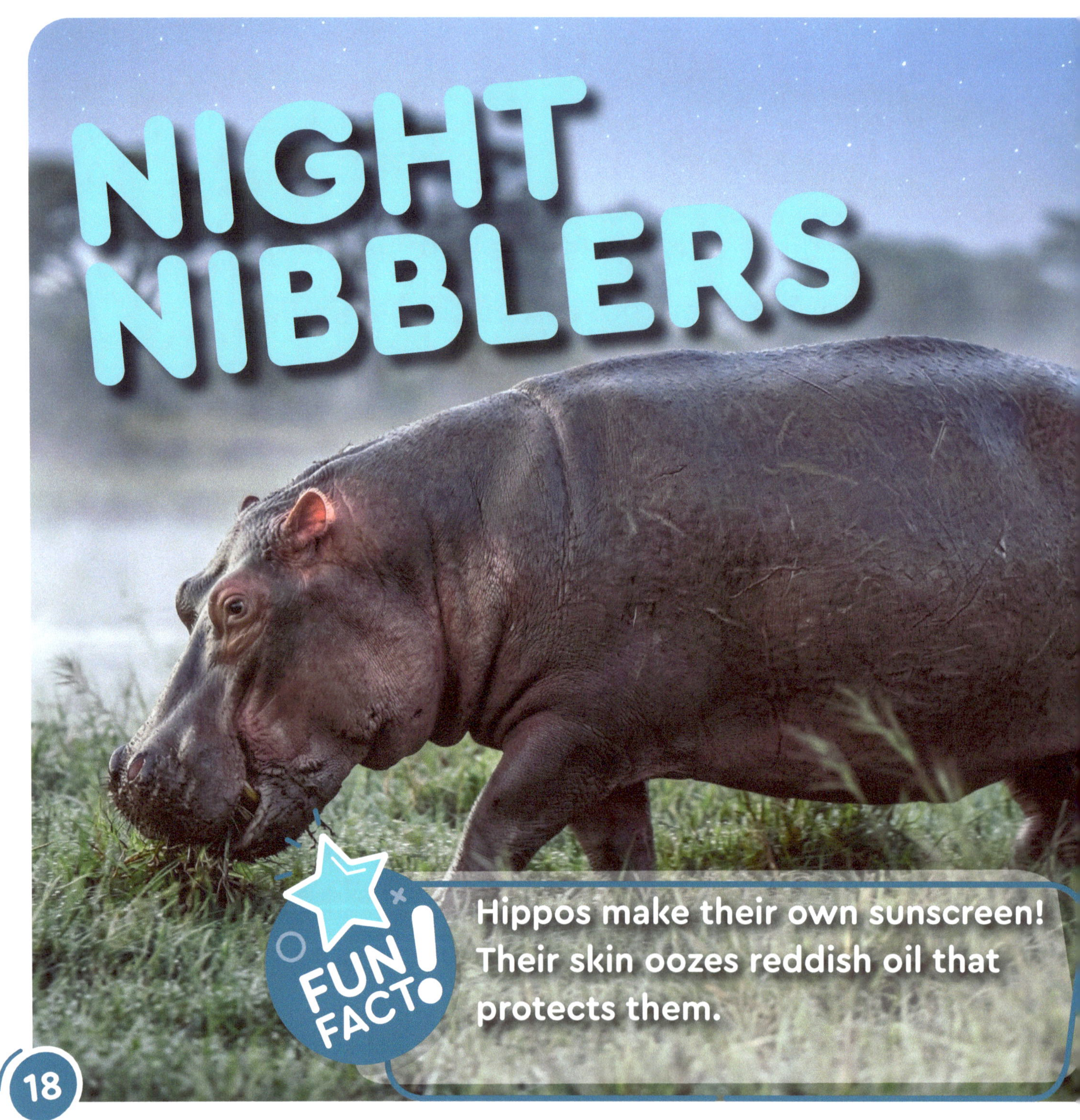

Hippos make their own sunscreen! Their skin oozes reddish oil that protects them.

Crunch! A hippo munches grass under the stars. Night is feeding time.

Hippos feed at night. They leave the water when the sun goes down. The cool night air also helps keep their skin moist.

Hippos walk to grassy areas near rivers. They may travel up to five miles to find food. Their wide paths through the grass are easy to spot. The same hippo often uses the same path over and over.

They spend about five hours eating each night. Then hippos return to the water before sunrise. This nighttime feeding keeps them cool. The hot African sun can dry out their skin.

WATCH OUT

A crocodile swims near a hippo. The hippo shows its big teeth.

Hippos look slow and calm. But they can be very dangerous. They are one of the most deadly animals in Africa.

Hippos do not like surprises. They may charge at boats that get too close. They can also run fast on land.

Crocodiles and lions sometimes attack young hippos. But adult hippos are usually too big to attack. These big hippos use their powerful jaws to defend themselves.

Hippos can open their mouths almost four feet wide to scare enemies.

SPLASH AWAY

Whoosh! A hippo dives under the water. It disappears fast!

Hippos often go underwater to stay cool and rest safely. They can hold their breath for up to five minutes.

Hippos sink to the bottom of rivers and lakes. They close their nostrils tight to keep water out.

Water is a hippo's safe place. Baby hippos are born underwater and can hold their breath right away.

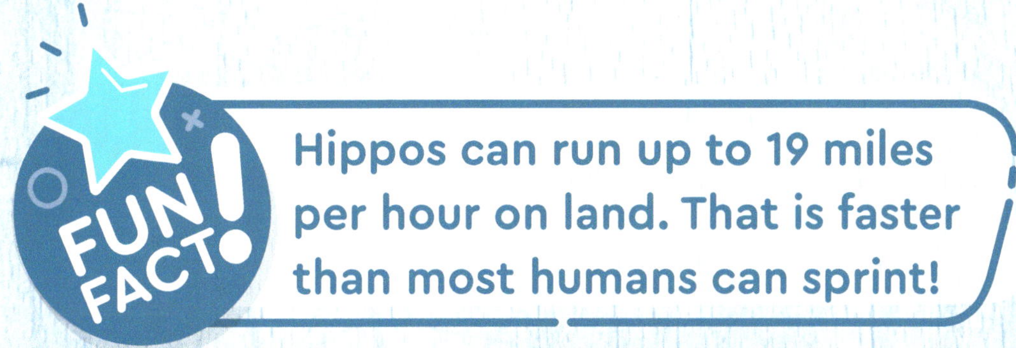

24

A baby hippo walks along the river bottom. Watch it glide!

Hippos are not great swimmers. Their bodies are too heavy to float. Instead, they walk or bounce along the bottom of rivers.

To move, hippos push off the ground with their strong legs. This lets them glide through the water in slow motion.

Baby hippos are born underwater and must swim to the surface for their first breath.

LAZY DAYS

Yawn! A hippo rests in shallow water. Its eyes look sleepy.

Hippos spend most of the day resting. They stay in water to keep cool. This protects them from the hot African sun.

Hippos often rest in groups. They lie close together in rivers and lakes. Sometimes they pile on top of each other!

Hippos even sleep in the water. Their bodies rise up to breathe without waking.

Hippos can spend up to 16 hours each day resting in the water before going out to eat at night.

BLOAT BUDDIES

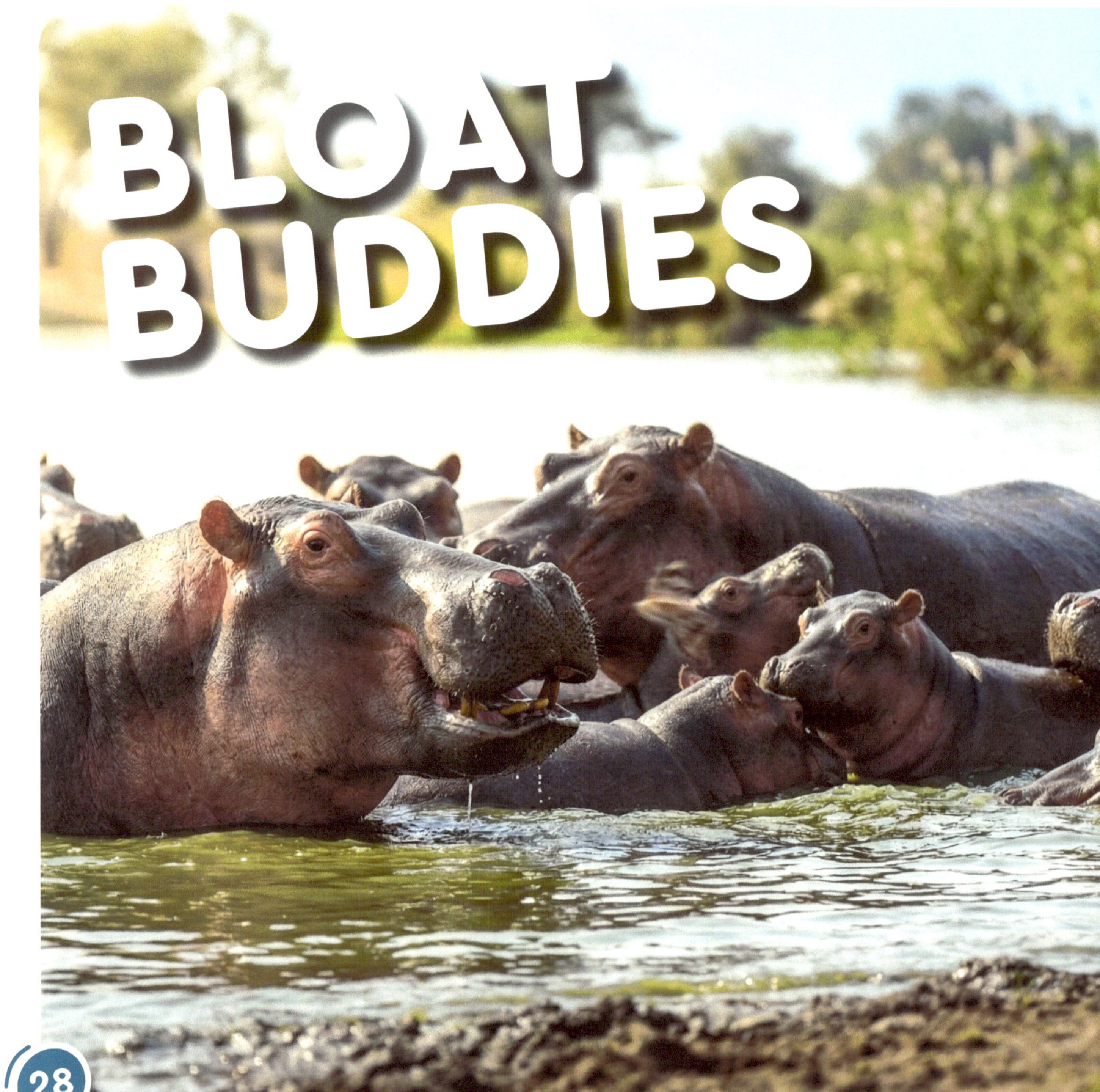

Squeeze! Many hippos crowd together in a river. What a group!

A group of hippos is called a bloat. Bloats can have 10 to 30 hippos. They all share the same stretch of water.

One big male leads each bloat. He watches over his area and keeps rival males out.

Mothers and babies stay close together in a group. This keeps them safe.

Hippos make loud honking sounds to talk to each other. These calls can be heard above and below water!

BIG BATTLES

Roar! Two male hippos charge at each other. Jaws open wide!

Male hippos fight to lead a bloat. They clash with their huge mouths open. Their long teeth can cause deep cuts.

Fights can last for hours. Males push and bite each other in the water. The winner gets to stay with the group.

Most fights end without serious harm. Usually, one male backs away. Then the stronger male takes charge.

Battle scars tell a hippo's story. Older males have deep marks from years of fighting.

CUTE CALVES
DID YOU KNOW?
Hippo calves gain about 10 pounds every day during their first year. They grow super fast and strong!

Squeak! A baby hippo pops up from the water. So cute!

A baby hippo is called a calf. Newborn calves weigh about 50 to 110 pounds. They can stand and walk soon after birth.

Calves are born underwater. They swim up to take their first breath. Then they start to nurse right away.

Young hippos grow fast. They drink their mother's milk for about eight months. Calves also start eating grass when they are a few weeks old.

Calves stay near their mothers for years.

MAMA KNOWS
DID YOU KNOW?
Mother hippos can carry their calves on their backs in deep water.
34

Nuzzle! A mother hippo nudges her calf to keep it close.

Mother hippos protect their calves fiercely. They chase away any animal that comes too close. Even crocodiles swim away from an angry mother.

Mothers teach their calves important skills. Young hippos learn where to find the best grass. They also learn safe paths to the water.

Calves follow their mothers everywhere. They copy what she does, and this helps them learn how to be hippos. Mothers and calves stay bonded for several years.

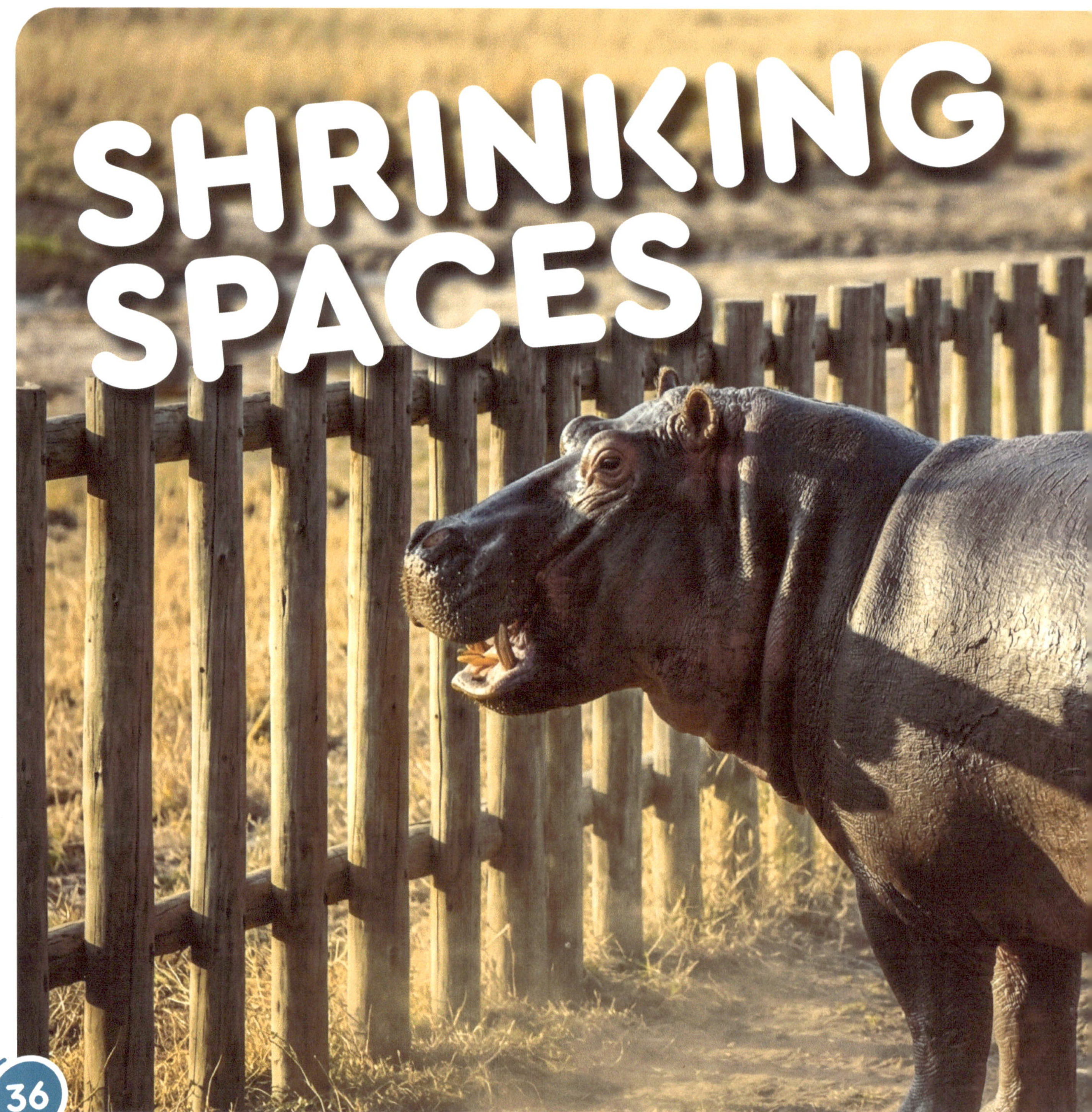

SHRINKING
SPACES
36

A fence blocks a hippo's path. The land beyond looks dry and empty.

Hippos need rivers, lakes, and grasslands. But people build farms and towns in these places. This leaves less space for hippos.

When land shrinks, hippos have trouble finding food and water. They may wander into villages looking for grass.

Rivers dry up when people take too much water. Hippos lose their homes.

Hippos help other animals. Their paths through tall grass create trails for smaller creatures to use.

HELPING
HIPPOS

Click! A scientist takes a photo of a hippo to help count them.

People work hard to save hippos. Scientists count hippos from planes and boats. This helps them know how many hippos live in each area.

Some countries create safe places for hippos. These protected areas keep rivers and grasslands healthy.

Groups teach farmers how to live near hippos safely. They build fences to protect crops.

Some zoos breed hippos to keep the species healthy. Zoo babies help protect hippos.

GLOSSARY

herbivores
Animals that eat only plants.

bloat
A group of hippos living together.

calf
A baby hippo.

membrane
A thin, clear covering that protects something.

glands
Body parts that make special liquids.

www.ingramcontent.com/pod-product-compliance
Lightning Source LLC
Chambersburg PA
CBHW041614110726
48005CB00002B/395